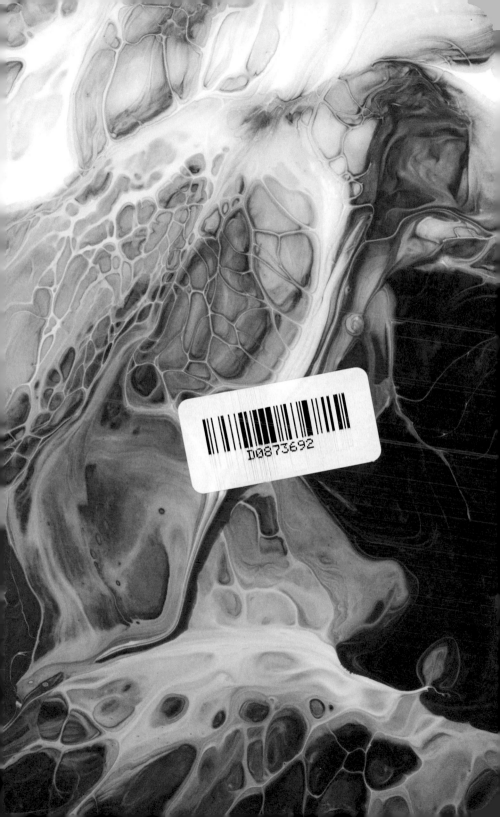

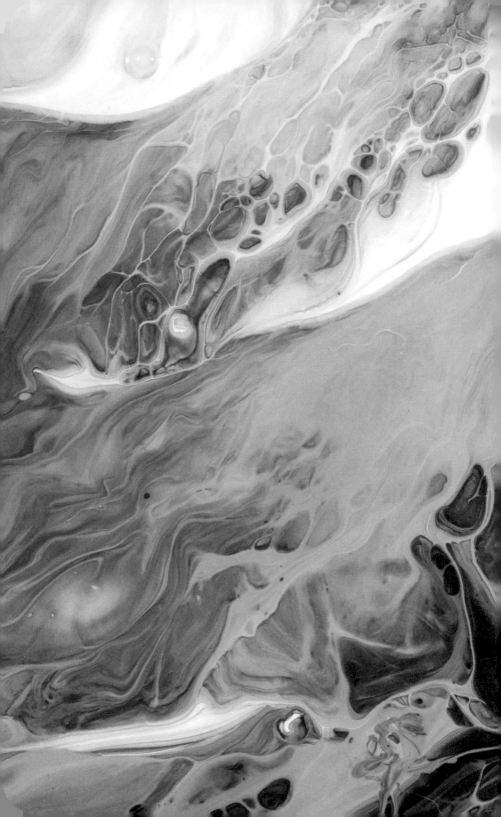

SUPERNATURAL BREAKTHROUGH

JOHN 14:12 ──────

SUPERNATURAL BREAKTHROUGH

JOHN 14:12 ——————

THOSE WHO BELIEVE WILL DO GREATER WORKS.

WHITAKER
HOUSE

This Supernatural Breakthrough Journal *belongs to:*

_____

THE SECRET PLACE—A PLACE OF SUPERNATURAL BREAKTHROUGH

God's presence is manifested to us in the secret place of prayer, where we come to know our heavenly Father. As we pray, God reveals Himself to us, and we are drawn to Him in ever greater ways. He places us under His care as His special treasure and part of His very heart.

The result is that *prayer in God's presence generates power*. When someone prays in the secret place, they are empowered to go and pour out that power upon other people for healing, deliverance, and miracles. Although power is our inheritance as children of God, we can only use it legally, in a spiritual sense, through prayer that is part of an intimate relationship with the Father.

Many people are being prevented from knowing God and accessing His presence and power for one reason—they have never developed a consistent prayer life. When continuity in prayer ceases, momentum in the Spirit is halted. But when we pray continuously, we generate a momentum that produces a prayer "accumulation" in the Spirit that builds to the point of breakthrough and victory.

This *Supernatural Breakthrough Journal* will be a tremendous blessing to you by helping you establish a lifestyle of continually walking in God's presence—boldly moving in the supernatural and bringing transformation to your life and the world around you. God answers the prayers of everyone who prays according to His will. Don't ever let yourself become discouraged if the answers to your prayers have not yet manifested. Keep praying, keep obeying, keep deepening your faith and trust, and keep building momentum—until you achieve an accumulation of prayers igniting your breakthrough!

Throughout this journal, you will find spiritual truths and principles of breakthrough drawn from a number of my books, with corresponding prayers and Scriptures. Use these as a starting point each day for entering God's presence, challenging your faith, and operating in the realm of the Spirit as you move from natural to supernatural. Record your personal prayers, revelations, and supernatural breakthroughs in these pages. Let them be a testimony of God's great love and power!

Each day, when you pray, remember to focus on God's priorities—what He says in His Word about His great purposes for the world, especially in these momentous end times. His priorities are that His kingdom be manifested on earth as it is in heaven; that people be saved, filled with His Spirit, healed, delivered, and commissioned to bring His gospel throughout the world; that miracles, signs, and wonders be demonstrated by His people, confirming the reality of the kingdom gospel; that families be reconciled and live together in love and peace; that the nations acknowledge His name; that His church be sanctified as the bride of Christ; and that *"the earth… be filled with the knowledge of the glory of the* LORD, *as the waters cover the sea"* (Habakkuk 2:14).

God wants you to have a part in these great purposes. Jesus has called us to continue His ministry on earth, saying, *"He that believes on Me, the works that I do shall he do also; and greater works than these shall he do; because I go to My Father"* (John 14:12). Those who believe will do *"greater works."* It all begins in the presence of God—surrendering to His will, being filled with His Spirit, exercising the faith He has given you, and obeying His leading. I declare that remarkable breakthroughs and supernatural demonstrations will be manifested through your life, and that you will fill these pages with testimonies and praises to the glory of God!

> Every prayer begins when we recognize we are in the presence of God. We start by acknowledging God's existence and qualities. This is the golden rule of prayer.

Holy, holy, holy, Lord God Almighty, which was, and is, and is to come.
(Revelation 4:8)

The LORD is gracious, and full of compassion; slow to anger, and of great mercy.
(Psalm 145:8)

> **A true relationship with God arises from a love that is birthed in the heart and that surrenders completely to the Beloved.**

You shall love the Lord your God with all your heart, and with all your soul, and with all your mind. (Matthew 22:37)

Prayer is the way through which the supernatural moves. For the church to continue being supernatural, it must maintain a life of prayer, fulfilling its purpose as a 'house of prayer.'

For My house shall be called a house of prayer for all nations.

(Isaiah 56:7 NKJV)

The highest level of prayer occurs when a believer becomes a house of prayer.

Father, in the name of Jesus, I ask that You would give me a spirit of prayer and a passion to be in Your presence and to be a house of prayer myself. I receive Your grace and the power of the Holy Spirit to pray Your perfect will, so that Your presence will flow in Your church—to heal, to do miracles, and to deliver Your people from demonic oppression, negative soul ties, and a lack of forgiveness. Starting today, in the name of Jesus and in the power of the Holy Spirit, I will be a house of prayer. Amen.

God's glory manifests where praise is high and worship is deep.

Whenever the living creatures give glory and honor and thanks to Him who sits on the throne, who lives forever and ever, the twenty-four elders fall down before Him who sits on the throne and worship Him who lives forever and ever, and cast their crowns before the throne, saying: "You are worthy, O Lord, to receive glory and honor and power; for You created all things, and by Your will they exist and were created."

(Revelation 4:9–11 NKJV)

> **In worship, when we exalt Christ's finished work on the cross, honor God's name, and extol His glory and majesty, He brings His power and presence into our midst here and now.**

[The disciples prayed,] "Lord,...grant to Your servants that with all boldness they may speak Your word, by stretching out Your hand to heal, and that signs and wonders may be done through the name of Your holy Servant Jesus." And when they had prayed, the place where they were assembled together was shaken; and they were all filled with the Holy Spirit, and they spoke the word of God with boldness.

(Acts 4:29–31 NKJV)

Worship establishes the divine atmosphere on earth.

[At the temple dedication, King Solomon] *said, O LORD God of Israel, there is no God like You in the heaven, nor in the earth; which keeps covenant, and shows mercy to Your servants, that walk before You with all their hearts.... Now when Solomon had made an end of praying, the fire came down from heaven, and consumed the burned offering and the sacrifices; and the glory of the LORD filled the house. And the priests could not enter into the house of the LORD, because the glory of the LORD had filled the LORD's house.* (2 Chronicles 6:14; 7:1–2)

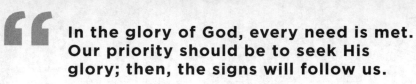

In the glory of God, every need is met. Our priority should be to seek His glory; then, the signs will follow us.

A prayer and declaration from Apostle Maldonado:

Heavenly Father, on behalf of this dear believer, I pray that You might open the eyes of their understanding and illuminate them with the spirit of wisdom and revelation, which will enable them to comprehend the mysteries of Your glory. I ask You to confirm this revelation by supernaturally manifesting in their lives right now. If they are sick, I ask that You heal them. If they are depressed or emotionally oppressed, I ask that You deliver them. If they need a creative miracle, I ask that they receive it right now. Manifest in their lives with miracles of supernatural provision. And for those who yearn to be transformed and to enter a greater dimension of glory, I release Your presence upon them right now! Manifest as the living and resurrected Christ. I believe with all my heart that You will do this. In the name of Jesus, amen!

The proof that we are praying in the presence of God is that we become carriers of His presence. The power of God that you carry will always be directly proportional to your prayer life.

And [Jesus] withdrew Himself into the wilderness, and prayed. And it came to pass on a certain day, as He was teaching, that there were Pharisees and doctors [teachers] of the law sitting by, which were come out of every town of Galilee, and Judaea, and Jerusalem: and the power of the Lord was present to heal them. (Luke 5:16–17)

The ingredients in the atmosphere of glory are continuous prayer, offerings, intercession, praise, worship, obedience, and honor.

Give to the LORD the glory due to His name: bring an offering, and come before Him: worship the LORD in the beauty of holiness.

(1 Chronicles 16:29)

High and spontaneous praise births supernatural breakthroughs.

So continuing daily with one accord in the temple, and breaking bread from house to house, they ate their food with gladness and simplicity of heart, praising God and having favor with all the people. And the Lord added to the church daily those who were being saved.

(Acts 2:46–47 NKJV)

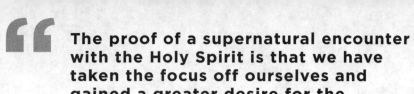

The proof of a supernatural encounter with the Holy Spirit is that we have taken the focus off ourselves and gained a greater desire for the presence of God.

Whom have I in heaven but You? and there is none upon earth that I desire beside You. My flesh and my heart fails: but God is the strength of my heart, and my portion for ever. (Psalm 73:25–26)

If we have yet to experience a breakthrough in an area where we need one, it could be that we lack hunger and thirst for God. Wherever there is a lack of hunger and thirst for God, the Lord has nothing to work with.

*As the deer pants for the water brooks, so pants my soul for You, O God.
My soul thirsts for God, for the living God.* (Psalm 42:1–2 NKJV)

Our true repentance always brings us back to the presence of God.

"

The sacrifices of God are a broken spirit: a broken and a contrite heart,
O God, You will not despise.   (Psalm 51:17)

Prayer for Salvation

If you recognize that you need God to change your heart and are willing to surrender your life to Him completely, pray the following prayer. Trust that God will help you to give all the areas of your life to Him as He transforms you, for *"the one who calls you is faithful, and he will do it"* (1 Thessalonians 5:24 NIV).

Heavenly Father, I recognize that I am a sinner and that my sin separates me from You. My heart is in need of transformation, which only You can accomplish. I believe that Jesus died on the cross for me and that You raised Him from the dead. I confess with my mouth that Jesus is Lord. I repent of all my sins and break every evil covenant I have made with the world, with my sinful nature, and with the devil. Now, I make a new covenant of righteousness with Jesus. I ask Jesus to come into my heart and to change my life, filling me with the Holy Spirit. If I were to die right now, I know I would be in Your presence when I opened my eyes in eternity. In Jesus's name, amen!

When the Holy Spirit manifests, there is life, and what's dead is raised again.

Heavenly Father, from this day forward, I surrender to You, and I ask You to rule over me and to live Your life through me. You resurrect my life, my vision, my dreams, my health, my home, and my finances. I am healed and free. I receive a creative miracle, right now! Jesus, I adore You because the impossible has become possible through Your resurrection. Thank You for making me a fellow heir with You of God's blessings. In Jesus's name, amen.

'Father,...You always hear Me'! (See John 11:41–42.) That is the level of prayer we can reach if we continually live in righteousness.

But you, when you pray, go into your room, and when you have shut your door, pray to your Father who is in the secret place; and your Father who sees in secret will reward you openly. (Matthew 6:6 NKJV)

" When we pray with the Word, we are praying the will of God. When His Word is the substance of our prayers, and we are in right relationship with Him, it commits Him to give us an answer. **"**

So shall My word be that goes forth out of My mouth: it shall not return to Me void, but it shall accomplish that which I please, and it shall prosper in the thing whereto I sent it. (Isaiah 55:11)

> **When continuity in prayer stops, momentum in the Spirit is halted. For a breakthrough to come upon a people or a nation, prayer accumulation is needed.**

A prayer and declaration from Apostle Maldonado:

Beloved heavenly Father, right now, I release Your supernatural grace upon this believer so that they may persevere in prayer until they see their breakthrough. I declare that every spirit of delay has been defeated, and that Your power is released upon them, in order to see Your will be fulfilled on earth as it is in heaven—with healings, miracles, signs, and wonders.

Receive this breakthrough now, in the name of Jesus! And when you have received it, maintain it by surrounding it with prayer so you will never lose it.

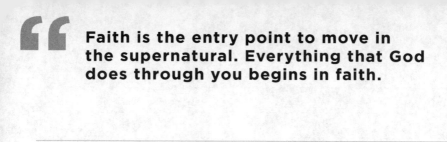

Faith is the entry point to move in the supernatural. Everything that God does through you begins in faith.

Without faith it is impossible to please Him: for he that comes to God must believe that He is, and that He is a rewarder of them that diligently seek Him. (Hebrews 11:6)

Prayer for Deliverance from the Spirit of Unbelief

Confess this prayer daily until every root of the spirit of unbelief in your heart has been pulled up and discarded:

Heavenly Father, thank You for opening my spiritual eyes and enabling me to see the unbelief in my heart. I praise You and bless You for teaching me how to be free of this rebellion against You and this resistance to Your will! In Christ, and with all my heart, I ask You to forgive me for having allowed my limited human reason and intellect to make me doubt You and Your promises, and for having permitted the spirit of unbelief to enter my life. Forgive me for making a "god" of my mind. Right now, I renounce the wicked spirit of unbelief, and, in the name of Jesus, I order it to leave my life.

Lord, I ask You, through Your Holy Spirit, to release the *"spirit of faith"* in me. "Baptize" me in faith to believe any portion of Your Word that I have previously found difficult to accept and receive—and to believe for even greater things! I receive Your faith right now. Help me to guard my heart and mind so that I will not allow unbelief to enter. I declare that everything that was held back in my life due to unbelief is now released. I receive my [salvation, healing, deliverance, financial provision, family restoration, or other blessing], in the name of Jesus. Amen! (See 2 Corinthians 4:13.)

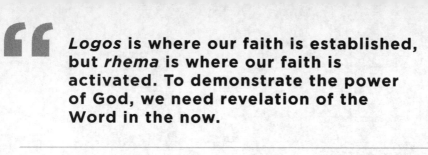

> **Logos** is where our faith is established, but **rhema** is where our faith is activated. To demonstrate the power of God, we need revelation of the Word in the now.

Father, please give me new revelation that will take me to another level of faith. Connect me with men and women who can release my faith, so I can bless other people, pray for the sick, and tend to those who need a touch of Your supernatural power. In Jesus's name, amen.

Faith is for now! This is the principle required to receive your miracle.

[Jesus said,] *Therefore I say to you, What things soever you desire, when you pray, believe that you receive them, and you shall have them.*

(Mark 11:24)

> **The cross is the basis on which God provides absolute and total provision to mankind.**

For you know the grace of our Lord Jesus Christ, that, though He was rich, yet for your sakes He became poor, that you through His poverty might be rich. (2 Corinthians 8:9)

Spiritual power and authority are obtained by submission to the lordship of Christ.

I am the vine, you are the branches: He that abides in Me, and I in him,
the same brings forth much fruit: for without Me you can do nothing.
(John 15:5)

The surrendering of our life to God is continuous and progressive.

Lord, I voluntarily crucify my flesh and deny myself. I take up my cross and follow You. I declare that the "old man" does not control my life. I submit my flesh to the finished work of Jesus on the cross and receive His grace to live in righteousness before You. I willingly choose to yield to Your Spirit rather than to the carnal nature. I pray this in the name of Jesus Christ, amen.

The purpose of Jesus's lordship over us is to transform our heart, so that He may manifest His life through us.

I am crucified with Christ: nevertheless I live; yet not I, but Christ lives in me: and the life which I now live in the flesh I live by the faith of the Son of God, who loved me, and gave Himself for me.   (Galatians 2:20)

> **The Christian life does not consist of struggling but of yielding. It is not an effort but a choice that comes from our union with the Holy Spirit.**

Father,…not My will, but Yours, be done. (Luke 22:42)

Prayer and Declaration from Apostle Maldonado to Receive the Baptism of the Holy Spirit

Dear friend, allow me the opportunity to pray for your life, so that the fire of the presence of God can come upon you, and you can begin to seek His face and His fire.

Heavenly Father, thank You for each person using this journal. I ask that those who have never been filled with power through the baptism of the Holy Spirit with the evidence of speaking in other tongues be filled right now. In Jesus's name, amen.

My advice to you is to open your mouth now and begin to speak the words the Holy Spirit gives you in other tongues. And, in the name of Jesus, I release the fire of the presence of God to everyone who hungers for it. I declare that you are submerged and ignited this instant. Receive it now and be filled with the power and fire! Have absolute faith and conviction that His fire is burning your interior at this instant. Once you are ignited—on fire—go as an instrument of the Lord and be a witness of Jesus. Call the lost to salvation, heal the sick, cast out demons, and deliver the captives. Amen!

**The more we humble ourselves,
the more power God will manifest
through us.**

Heavenly Father, I humble myself before You in the name of Jesus. I repent of my sins of commission and omission [name specifically] and turn from all ways that do not honor You. I declare myself free from them, and I will passionately seek You and experience Your presence. In Jesus's name, amen!

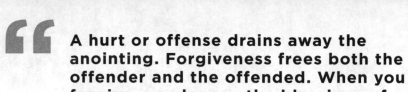

A hurt or offense drains away the anointing. Forgiveness frees both the offender and the offended. When you forgive, you loosen the blessings of God on your behalf.

If you forgive men their trespasses, your heavenly Father will also forgive you: but if you forgive not men their trespasses, neither will your Father forgive your trespasses. (Matthew 6:14–15)

Prayer of Forgiveness

Heavenly Father, I come before Your presence recognizing my need to forgive. With all my heart, I repent for harboring unforgiveness toward other people—and myself—thus breaking Your law. I freely submit to You and Your Word. I believe You are willing to forgive me for my bitterness and unforgiveness, and that Jesus Christ made this possible through His death on the cross. I receive His work on my behalf, which has loosed me not only to be forgiven but also to forgive others. Jesus carried my sins so I could be forgiven; and, right now, I make a decision to forgive these people: _____ [identify them by name and specifically mention their offense]. Lord, right now, I forgive all who have hurt me, just as You have forgiven me for my sins and continue to forgive me when I sin against You. I trust in Your supernatural grace to enable me to fully forgive and release all who have offended me. I affirm that I have forgiven them and that I have been forgiven. Thank You, Lord. In Jesus's name, amen.

Prayer from Apostle Maldonado

Father, in the name of Jesus, I tear out all roots of unforgiveness from the heart of this believer. I deliver them from any spirit of hatred, resentment, bitterness, hurt, anger, fear, suffering, or disease. I bind these spirits and cast them out in the name of Jesus, never to return. I cancel all demonic assignments, bonds, oppression, spiritual influences, and power right now, in the name of Jesus. The "tree" of unforgiveness is dead and can never again bear fruit. I now release the power of Christ's blood over His child. I declare that they are healthy and free, having supernatural grace to fully forgive and to live the life You intended. In Jesus's name, amen.

> **The believer who wants to be a chosen vessel to carry the glory of God must cross over the lines of comfort, convenience, and human reason.**

I also count all things loss for the excellence of the knowledge of Christ Jesus my Lord, for whom I have suffered the loss of all things, and count them as rubbish, that I may gain Christ and be found in Him, not having my own righteousness, which is from the law, but that which is through faith in Christ, the righteousness which is from God by faith; that I may know Him and the power of His resurrection, and the fellowship of His sufferings, being conformed to His death. (Philippians 3:8–10 NKJV)

> **Those who are able to carry something real from God to others have begun with sacrifice—such as fasting, prayer, and seeking God.**

As they [the prophets and teachers at Antioch] *ministered to the Lord and fasted, the Holy Spirit said, "Now separate to Me Barnabas and Saul for the work to which I have called them." Then, having fasted and prayed, and laid hands on them, they sent them away.*

(Acts 13:2–3 NKJV)

My food is to do the will of Him who sent Me, and to finish His work.
(John 4:34 NKJV)

> **The main purpose of revelation is to lead us to a supernatural experience in God's presence so that we can be transformed.**

That the God of our Lord Jesus Christ, the Father of glory, may give to you the spirit of wisdom and revelation in the knowledge of Him: the eyes of your understanding being enlightened; that you may know what is the hope of His calling, and what the riches of the glory of His inheritance in the saints, and what is the exceeding greatness of His power to us-ward who believe, according to the working of His mighty power.

(Ephesians 1:17–19)

No knowledge or revelation becomes ours until it is obeyed and practiced.

Be doers of the word, and not hearers only, deceiving yourselves.... He who looks into the perfect law of liberty and continues in it, and is not a forgetful hearer but a doer of the work, this one will be blessed in what he does. (James 1:22, 25 NKJV)

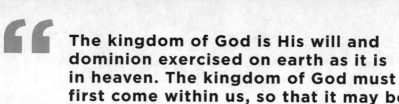

> **The kingdom of God is His will and dominion exercised on earth as it is in heaven. The kingdom of God must first come within us, so that it may be manifested externally.**

Heavenly Father, I am Your beloved child. I am a king and priest under Your authority who rules over my territory in Your kingdom. I am a warrior, having Your spirit of might to break down Satan's walls of containment and receive Your breakthroughs for the greater expansion of Your kingdom. Live in me today, and let Your Spirit move in my life. Let my heart always be receptive and obedient to Your purpose and will. May Your kingdom come and Your will be done on earth as it is in heaven—in the here and now, and for all eternity. Amen and amen!

> **Genuine love must dwell within us if we are to demonstrate that love to others.**

The love of God has been poured out in our hearts by the Holy Spirit who was given to us. (Romans 5:5 NKJV)

> **Many people do not want to hear a message—they want to see one.**

And they went forth, and preached every where, the Lord working with them, and confirming the word with signs following.   (Mark 16:20)

Be imitators of God as dear children. And walk in love, as Christ also has loved us and given Himself for us, an offering and a sacrifice to God for a sweet-smelling aroma.   (Ephesians 5:1–2 NKJV)

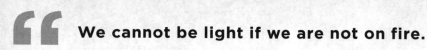
We cannot be light if we are not on fire.

You are the light of the world. A city that is set on a hill cannot be hidden. Nor do they light a lamp and put it under a basket, but on a lampstand, and it gives light to all who are in the house. Let your light so shine before men, that they may see your good works and glorify your Father in heaven. (Matthew 5:14–16 NKJV)

Our faithfulness and stewardship determine the level to which our blessings will increase.

Behold, a sower went forth to sow; and when he sowed,…some fell among thorns; and the thorns sprung up, and choked them: but other fell into good ground, and brought forth fruit, some a hundredfold, some sixty-fold, some thirtyfold. (Matthew 13:3–4, 7–8)

If it offends you to give to God, then it should also offend you to receive from Him.

Do not worry, saying, "What shall we eat?" or "What shall we drink?"
or "What shall we wear?" For after all these things the Gentiles seek. For
your heavenly Father knows that you need all these things. But seek first
the kingdom of God and His righteousness, and all these things shall be
added to you. (Matthew 6:31–33 NKJV)

> **Mental strongholds are formed when we accept, and come into one accord with, false and negative arguments, reasonings, and imaginations. A mind that has not been renewed will repeat negative cycles of thinking.**

Be not conformed to this world: but be you transformed by the renewing of your mind, that you may prove what is that good, and acceptable, and perfect, will of God. (Romans 12:2)

Prayer for the Renewal of the Mind

Heavenly Father, thank You for the revelation You have given me through Your Word about how my mind can be renewed. Today, I want a radical change in my life. I repent of living according to the mentality of this world and of gratifying the sinful nature. I renounce the negative influences of the world, including "religion" and the limitations of human knowledge and reason. I want Your mind, Lord. I want Your way of thinking. I want Your supernatural mind-set. I surrender my mind and my thoughts to Your supernatural power, so that they can be exchanged for Your mind and thoughts. Please renew my mind, so that I can become a useful instrument in Your hands for Your kingdom and can take this revelation to other people who are trapped in the same condition I have been in. In the name of Jesus, I thank You for hearing me and for activating Your supernatural power over my life—here and now. In Jesus's name, amen.

Made the decision to remove all
boundaries that were unfair or unjust,
based on human reason.

Make the decision to remove all limitations you have placed on God based on human reason.

With men it is impossible, but not with God: for with God all things are possible. (Mark 10:27)

The only ability God seeks in mankind is availability.

I heard the voice of the Lord, saying, Whom shall I send, and who will go for Us? Then said I, Here am I; send me. (Isaiah 6:8)

Transitions are birthed in the midst of spiritual dissatisfaction and frustration. The spiritual hunger inside you is evidence that God is calling you to a greater dimension.

O God, You are my God; early will I seek You; my soul thirsts for You;
my flesh longs for You in a dry and thirsty land where there is no water.
So I have looked for You in the sanctuary, to see Your power and Your
glory. (Psalm 63:1–2 NKJV)

Prayer of Recommitment and Consecration to God

Jesus Christ, You are Lord. You are God's Son and the only way to the Father. You died for my sins and were raised from the dead on the third day. You purchased me with Your blood and transferred me from the kingdom of darkness into Your glorious kingdom of light. You freed me from slavery to Satan and enabled me to be reborn as a child of God. Now I recommit myself to You. I am willing to crucify my flesh and stand in the authority You gave me. I place myself at Your disposal. Do with me as You wish. Send me wherever You want me to go. From this day forward, You are my Lord, and I, of my own free will, submit to Your kingdom. Everything I do will be in obedience to Your Word and Your kingdom. I will no longer rule myself. Thank You for accepting this covenant of commitment. I know that I am not worthy, but Your blood makes me worthy. I am accepted. I am Your child! Anoint me with power to go and expand Your kingdom and to do warfare against the kingdom of darkness and destroy the works of the devil. Wherever I go, I will proclaim and demonstrate the gospel of Your kingdom to those who have yet to hear it and see it. Here I am, Lord—send me!

In the realm of prayer, natural laws can be put on hold and spiritual laws can take over.

Our Father in heaven, hallowed be Your name. Your kingdom come. Your will be done on earth as it is in heaven. (Luke 11:2 NKJV)

> **Intercessors rule on earth from the spirit realm. Declaring by faith, from eternity, brings things into existence.**

Heavenly Father, I pray from heaven to earth, which is the position that Christ won for us through His work at the cross. My faith is now, and all that You have spoken in heaven, I speak on earth, declaring that Your promises and mighty works come into existence in my life, in my family, in my ministry, in my nation, in Your church, and in all Your children. I speak Your will for Your kingdom to come on earth as it is in heaven. I declare there is supernatural grace for Your children to attain Your promises, expand Your kingdom, and preach Your gospel throughout the world! I pray all this in the name that is above all names—the name of Jesus. Amen!

> **The amount of revelation an individual has determines the level of faith in which he can operate.**

Faith comes by hearing, and hearing by the word of God.
(Romans 10:17)

Faith is the currency of the supernatural in the now.

"

Faith is the substance of things hoped for, the evidence of things not seen.
(Hebrews 11:1)

When we have God's faith, His Word in our mouths is the same as it is in His mouth.

If you abide in Me, and My words abide in you, you will ask what you desire, and it shall be done for you. By this My Father is glorified, that you bear much fruit; so you will be My disciples. (John 15:7–8 NKJV)

Faith acts and stands on what God has already predetermined, generating expectation.

[Abraham] *staggered not at the promise of God through unbelief; but was strong in faith, giving glory to God; and being fully persuaded that, what He had promised, He was able also to perform.*

(Romans 4:20–21)

> Words cannot replace actions, or actions replace words; both are necessary to demonstrate the power of God.

For as the body without the spirit is dead, so faith without works is dead also. (James 2:26)

God's supernatural grace enables us to do what we can't do in our own strength.

Dear Jesus, I am willing and available to go and demonstrate Your kingdom here and now. I ask You to give me Your supernatural grace to take risks and be bold in order to manifest Your power and glory. I ask Your Holy Spirit to come upon me and empower me now to do the works of the kingdom. By faith, wherever I go—to my school, my job, a restaurant, a sporting event, the mall, or anywhere else—I will pray for the sick, the oppressed, and the captives, and I will deliver them in Your name. Those who haven't received salvation or the baptism in the Holy Spirit will receive it by Your power! I submit my will and my heart to You right now. In Your name, amen.

Faith 'sees' the invisible, believes the incredible, and receives the impossible.

If then you were raised with Christ, seek those things which are above, where Christ is, sitting at the right hand of God. Set your mind on things above, not on things on the earth. (Colossians 3:1–2 NKJV)

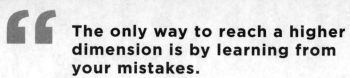

The only way to reach a higher dimension is by learning from your mistakes.

And [Jesus] said, Come. And when Peter was come down out of the ship, he walked on the water, to go to Jesus. But when he saw the wind boisterous, he was afraid; and beginning to sink, he cried, saying, Lord, save me. And immediately Jesus stretched forth His hand, and caught him, and said to him, O you of little faith, wherefore did you doubt?

(Matthew 14:29–31)

> One of God's smallest creations is a seed that has the potential to grow into a great tree. Everything God creates has the potential to grow and to multiply.

The kingdom of heaven is like to a grain of mustard seed, which a man took, and sowed in his field: which indeed is the least of all seeds: but when it is grown, it is the greatest among herbs, and becomes a tree, so that the birds of the air come and lodge in the branches thereof.

(Matthew 13:31–32)

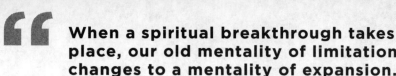

> When a spiritual breakthrough takes place, our old mentality of limitation changes to a mentality of expansion.

Enlarge the place of your tent, and let them stretch forth the curtains of your habitations: spare not, lengthen your cords, and strengthen your stakes. (Isaiah 54:2)

Every miracle and healing that Jesus performed was motivated by compassion.

Now when [Jesus] came near to the gate of the city, behold, there was a dead man carried out, the only son of his mother, and she was a widow.... And when the Lord saw her, He had compassion on her, and said to her, Weep not. And He came and touched the bier: and they that bore him stood still. And He said, Young man, I say to you, Arise. And he that was dead sat up, and began to speak. And He delivered him to his mother. (Luke 7:12–15)

By way of the cross, Jesus inflicted on Satan a total, permanent, eternal, and irrevocable defeat.

Every believer has t owering authority over Satan and his works

Having disarmed principalities and powers, He made a public spectacle of them, triumphing over them in it. (Colossians 2:15 NKJV)

Every believer has power and authority over Satan and his works.

And [Jesus] *said to them, "I saw Satan fall like lightning from heaven. Behold, I give you the authority to trample on serpents and scorpions, and over all the power of the enemy, and nothing shall by any means hurt you."* (Luke 10:18–19 NKJV)

Healing is a legal right that belongs to the believer—both to receive and to impart to others.

He was wounded for our transgressions, He was bruised for our iniquities: the chastisement of our peace was upon Him; and with His stripes we are healed. (Isaiah 53:5)

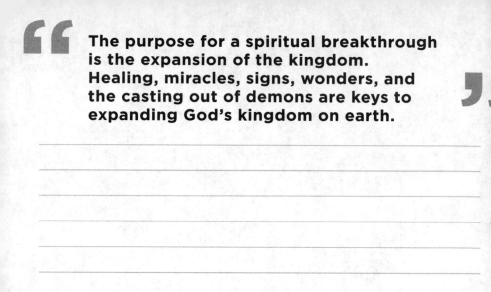

> **The purpose for a spiritual breakthrough is the expansion of the kingdom. Healing, miracles, signs, wonders, and the casting out of demons are keys to expanding God's kingdom on earth.**

Jesus answered and said to them, "Go and tell John the things you have seen and heard: that the blind see, the lame walk, the lepers are cleansed, the deaf hear, the dead are raised, the poor have the gospel preached to them." (Luke 7:22 NKJV)

If I cast out demons by the Spirit of God, surely the kingdom of God has come upon you. (Matthew 12:28 NKJV)

Prayer is the place where we obtain power in greater levels to deal with demons of greater rank.

,,

Then the disciples came to Jesus privately and said, "Why could we not cast [the demon] out?" So Jesus said to them, "Because of your unbelief; for assuredly, I say to you, if you have faith as a mustard seed, you will say to this mountain, 'Move from here to there,' and it will move; and nothing will be impossible for you. However, this kind does not go out except by prayer and fasting." (Matthew 17:19–21 NKJV)

The enemy seeks to infiltrate a mind that has not yet decided to believe or commit itself to what God has said.

Let him ask in faith, nothing wavering. For he that wavers [or doubts] is like a wave of the sea driven with the wind and tossed. For let not that man think that he shall receive any thing of the Lord. A double minded man is unstable in all his ways. (James 1:6–8)

> **The condition for subduing Satan and his demons is to remain in supernatural power and authority.**

When a strong man, fully armed, guards his own house, his possessions are safe. But when someone stronger attacks and overpowers him, he takes away the armor in which the man trusted and divides up his plunder.   (Luke 11:21–22 NIV)

Prayer to Be Free of Generational Curses

Heavenly Father, I praise and adore You. Thank You for Jesus Christ and for the finished work of the cross. I recognize that Jesus paid the price for my rebellion and my transgressions so that I could be free from the curse of iniquity. Today, I go to the cross to take hold of all the blessings that Christ legally won.

Lord Jesus, I believe You are the Son of God and the only way to heaven. I believe that You died for my sins and rose from the dead. As it says in Galatians, You "became a curse" on the cross so that I might be redeemed from the curse of the fall and all its ramifications. I receive my blessing, and from now on I commit to obey Your Word and to follow You all the days of my life, according to the power of the Holy Spirit. I ask for forgiveness for every sin committed by my ancestors that has led to a generational curse [mention all the generational curses you may have identified: sickness, depression, alcoholism, adultery, suicide, premature death, and anything else]. I also release all who have wronged me or committed evil against me. I forgive them as You have forgiven me.

Heavenly Father, I renounce any participation I have had in the practice of witchcraft, the occult, and idolatry, as well as any soul ties or spiritual links with others who have practiced these things. If I own any objects that are connected with these practices, I promise to destroy them right away. Now Lord, I take the authority and power that You have given me as Your child, and I release myself from every curse that has ever come to me. I rebuke and cast out every demon behind any of those curses. I remove all iniquity from within me. I declare myself free. Today, by the blood of Jesus, I am released from all generational curses. In Jesus's name, amen.

_____

_____

_____

_____

_____

_____

> The curse resulting from the fall of mankind includes sin, sickness, and poverty. To be under a curse is to be supernaturally empowered to fail. To be blessed is to be supernaturally empowered to prosper and have success against all odds and adversity.

_____

_____

_____

_____

_____

_____

_____

_____

_____

_____

_____

_____

_____

_____

_____

_____

_____

_____

_____

_____

_____

Blessed be the God and Father of our Lord Jesus Christ, who has blessed us with every spiritual blessing in the heavenly places in Christ.

(Ephesians 1:3 NKJV)

The blessing of God has the power to accelerate us in every area of life and to enable us to bless others.

The LORD had said to Abram,…. I will make of you a great nation, and I will bless you, and make your name great; and you shall be a blessing.

(Genesis 12:1–2)

> **The Holy Spirit goes where He is welcome, remains where He is recognized, and moves where He is given freedom.**

Holy Spirit, I make room for You to move freely in my life.

> **The only movement able to generate transformation in society is the outpouring of the glory of God.**

I saw also the LORD sitting upon a throne, high and lifted up, and His train filled the temple. Above it stood the seraphims: each one had six wings; with two he covered his face, and with two he covered his feet, and with two he did fly. And one cried to another, and said, Holy, holy, holy, is the LORD of hosts: the whole earth is full of His glory. (Isaiah 6:1–3)

You will experience the power and the glory of God only as you *'go into all the world.'* (See Mark 16:15.)

Heavenly Father, in the name of Jesus, I ask You to use me as a vessel of clay chosen to manifest Your glory as I live my life. I ask You to release the fire of Your presence in me, right now, so I will never again be a passive Christian but an active and daring one. Give me boldness, Lord. Let Your glory be upon me, every day of my life. I want to be a part of the remnant You are raising to manifest the latter glory. I receive it right now, and I go to my "world," in the name of Jesus. Amen!

> **In the move of the latter glory, the weakest believer will be like David, and the whole church united in Christ will be like God.**

Thanks be to God who always leads us in triumph in Christ, and through us diffuses the fragrance of His knowledge in every place.

(2 Corinthians 2:14 NKJV)

> The resurrection life that flows through us is supernatural by nature and origin. Miracles, signs, wonders, and the raising of the dead should be the norm for us.

Heavenly Father, I acknowledge that the power of the resurrection is available and active through me wherever I go. I can do all things through Christ who strengthens me! Nothing is impossible for me, as nothing is impossible for God. I am an extension of the resurrected Christ on earth in order to advance His kingdom. He lives, and I live according to His life and faith. Amen!

Christ's command was to *'watch and pray.'* We must watch and pray until He returns.

_____

_____

_____

_____

_____

_____

_____

_____

_____

_____

_____

_____

_____

_____

_____

_____

_____

_____

_____

_____

_____

[Jesus said,] *What, could you not watch with Me one hour? Watch and pray, that you enter not into temptation: the spirit indeed is willing, but the flesh is weak.* (Matthew 26:40–41)

Praying always with all prayer and supplication in the Spirit, being watchful to this end with all perseverance and supplication for all the saints. (Ephesians 6:18 NKJV)

> **The devil can attack your life only when you don't watch, because what you anticipate, you can prevent.**

Be sober, be vigilant; because your adversary the devil walks about like a roaring lion, seeking whom he may devour. Resist him, steadfast in the faith, knowing that the same sufferings are experienced by your brother-hood in the world. (1 Peter 5:8–9 NKJV)

Prayer for Deliverance from Demonic Oppression

Below is a list of conditions that will help you to be free of all demonic oppression operating in your mind, will, emotions, and body. To receive deliverance—and to stay free—you must:

- Have a personal revelation of Jesus as Lord and Savior.

- Humble yourself before God (those who refuse to humble themselves should not continue with the deliverance).

- Confess all sins of commission and omission.

- Repent wholeheartedly.

- Choose to forgive everyone who has offended you.

- Desperately desire your deliverance from the enemy's oppression.

- Break any pacts you have made with the occult through witchcraft, Santeria, or any other false religion or sect.

- Believe, confess, and receive, by faith, the divine exchange that took place at the cross of Christ.

- Exhale, so that every evil spirit can leave your body.

You may use the following prayer as a guide. It will keep you from forgetting any important aspects of deliverance.

Dear Lord, I believe that You are the Son of God and that You died on the cross for my sins; that You were raised from the dead so I could be forgiven and receive eternal life. Right now, I take hold of Your work and renounce all religious self-righteousness and any other sense of pride that does not come from You. I ask for Your mercy and grace, knowing that I have nothing to boast about. I wholeheartedly repent of and confess all the sins I have committed, as well as everything I should have done but failed to do. I choose to end my sinful lifestyle so that I may have new life in You. Of my own free will, I make a decision to follow You. I forgive everyone who has hurt me and has wished me harm. I renounce and let go of all unforgiveness, bitterness, hatred, and resentment. I specifically forgive [mention the names of those who have hurt you], and I ask for Your supernatural grace to forgive them.

I renounce every pact I have made with the occult, including witchcraft, divination, and false doctrines or religions. I also commit myself to destroying every object in my home or office that is associated with the occult and idolatry.

Lord Jesus, thank You for taking my curse on the cross so I could receive Your blessing. I am redeemed and free in Your name. I stand with You against Satan and his demons. I renounce the curses I have seen in operation in my life [mention all the generational curses you may have identified: sickness, depression, alcoholism, adultery, suicide, premature death, and anything else]. Now, I receive Your blessings. I resist the devil and submit to You. I order every demon that has control over my life, health, finances, and family to leave, right now! I cast them out, now, in the name of Jesus. I am free!

> **The baptism of the Holy Spirit happens once, but being filled should be repeated as many times as we need it. While we serve God, we will always have the need to be filled and to remain filled with Him.**

Heavenly Father, I have been fighting the enemy, sowing, praying for the sick, and preaching the Word, but it has been a long time since I was filled by Your Spirit. I have been leaking in my spirit, and today I need You to fill me again. I ask in the name of Jesus for a fresh outpouring, because I desperately need to be filled with the Holy Spirit. Amen.

A person whose imagination is based on faith lives each day with a new expectation.

And Peter, fastening his eyes upon him with John, said, Look on us. And he gave heed to them, expecting to receive something of them. Then Peter said, Silver and gold have I none; but such as I have give I you: In the name of Jesus Christ of Nazareth rise up and walk. (Acts 3:4–6)

You cannot carry a revival you do not participate in. That is why you need to jump into the river of the Spirit!

Whosoever drinks of the water that I shall give him shall never thirst; but the water that I shall give him shall be in him a well of water springing up into everlasting life. (John 4:14)

And the Spirit and the bride say, Come. And let him that hears say, Come. And let him that is thirsty come. And whosoever will, let him take the water of life freely. (Revelation 22:17)

Prayer and Declaration of Blessing from Apostle Maldonado

As an apostle, a pastor, and a spiritual father in the church of Jesus Christ, I want to bless you. Receive this prayer and declaration:

Heavenly Father, I come before Your presence according to the merits of Your Son Jesus Christ. Thank You for the many blessings You have given me so that I can be a blessing to others. What You have freely given me, I freely give to others. Therefore, to this believer, whom You love, I say, "I bless you, and I remove every curse and every negative word that anyone has been spoken against your life. And now, as an authority in the church of Christ, I release God's blessing into your life, and I empower you to prosper. I declare that everything you touch will be successful, and that the favor and grace of God will accompany you. I declare that you will succeed despite any negative or challenging circumstances. May the Lord release over you all the blessings that Jesus won on the cross. I declare that you are blessed with health in your body, health in your mind, and health in your soul. You will be fruitful, and you will multiply wherever you go. Against all odds, I declare that you are blessed and prosperous." In Jesus's name, amen!

This journal contains excerpts from the following books by Apostle Guillermo Maldonado: *Breakthrough Prayer, How to Walk in the Supernatural Power of God, The Glory of God, The Kingdom of Power, Supernatural Transformation, Supernatural Deliverance,* and *Divine Encounter with the Holy Spirit.* All excerpts © Guillermo Maldonado. All rights reserved.

SUPERNATURAL BREAKTHROUGH JOURNAL

Guillermo Maldonado
14100 SW 144th Ave.
Miami, FL 33186
King Jesus Ministry / ERJ Publicaciones
www.kingjesus.org
www.ERJPub.org

ISBN: 978-1-64123-163-3
Printed in the United States of America
© 2018 by Guillermo Maldonado

Whitaker House
1030 Hunt Valley Circle
New Kensington, PA 15068
www.whitakerhouse.com

1 2 3 4 5 6 7 8 9 10 11 12 ⨆⨆ 25 24 23 22 21 20 19 18

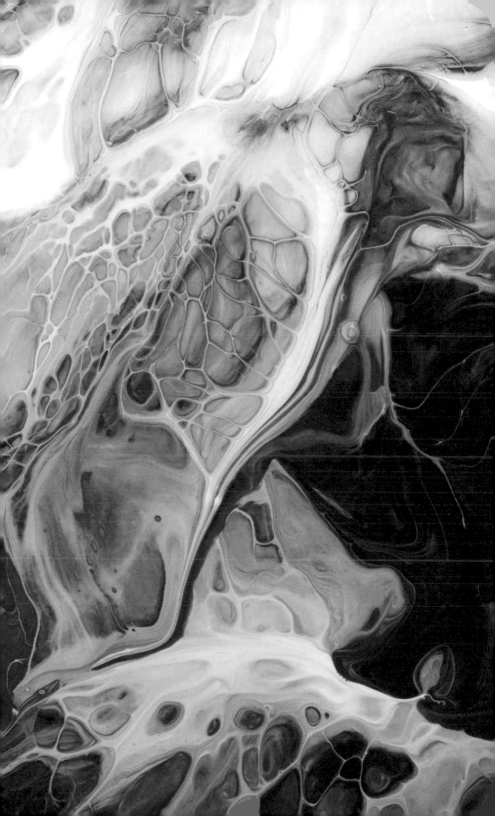

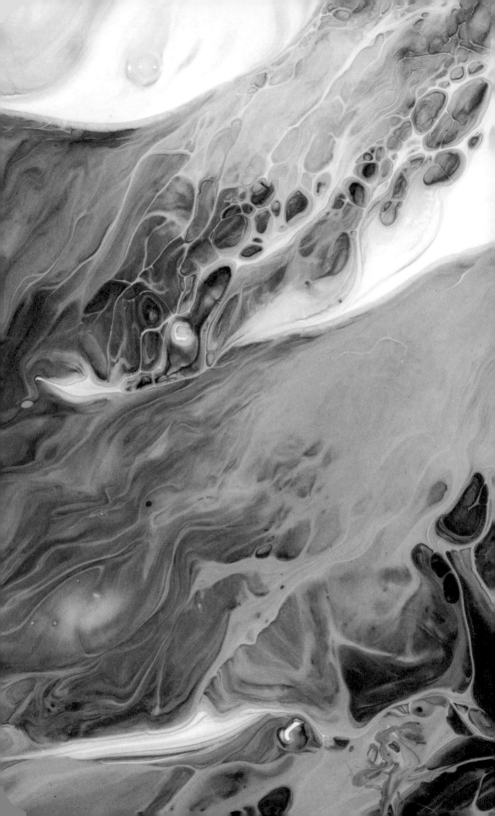